BIRDS ON STAGE

Written by Saturnino Romay   Illustrated by Claude Martinot

SCHOLASTIC INC.

New York   Toronto   London   Auckland   Sydney

Copyright © 1994 by Scholastic Inc.
All rights reserved. Published by Scholastic Inc.
Printed in the U.S.A.
ISBN 0-590-27379-5

3 4 5 6 7 8 9 10   08   00 99 98 97 96 95 94

This bird is as green as a pea.
When it flies, it hums like a bee.
What can it be?

A hummingbird.

This bird has an egg like a ball.

It's the biggest bird of them all.

What can it be?

An ostrich.

This bird loves the cold and the snow.
It looks like it's all dressed for a show.
What can it be?

A penguin.

This bird has a pretty surprise.
When it fans out its tail, the feathers
have eyes. What can it be?

A peacock.

This bird is as pink as pink roses.

It stands on one leg when it dozes.

What can it be?

A flamingo.

This bird has a beak half its size.
It's a wonder this bird ever flies.
What can it be?

A toucan.

This bird has a beak curved for cracking.
It likes to eat crackers when it's snacking.
What can it be?

A parrot.